D1712530

NATURE'S GROSSEST

LIZARD BLOOD

By Roberto Betances

Gareth Stevens
PUBLISHING

Please visit our website, www.garethstevens.com. For a free color catalog of all our high-quality books, call toll free 1-800-542-2595 or fax 1-877-542-2596.

Library of Congress Cataloging-in-Publication Data

Betances, Roberto.
Lizard blood / by Roberto Betances.
p. cm. — (Nature's grossest)
Includes index.
ISBN 978-1-4824-1841-5 (pbk.)
ISBN 978-1-4824-1842-2 (6-pack)
ISBN 978-1-4824-1843-9 (library binding)
1. Lizards — Juvenile literature. 2. Reptiles — Juvenile literature. I. Title.
QL666.L2 B48 2015
597.9—d23

Published in 2015 by
Gareth Stevens Publishing
111 East 14th Street, Suite 349
New York, NY 10003

Designer: Katelyn E. Reynolds
Editor: Therese Shea

Photo credits: Cover, p. 1 John Cancalosi/Photolibrary/Getty Images; pp. 3–24 (background) Oleksii Natykach/Shutterstock.com; p. 5 (gecko) nico99/Shutterstock.com; p. 5 (chameleon) Mark Bridger/Shutterstock.com; p. 5 (basilisk) fivespots/Shutterstock.com; p. 7 Jill Lang/ Shutterstock.com; pp. 9, 21 Matt Jeppson/Shutterstock.com; p. 11 Doug Steakley/Lonely Planet Images/Getty Images; p. 13 (blood splatter) M.E. Mulder/Shutterstock.com; p. 13 (lizard) Brian Lasenby/Shutterstock.com; pp. 15, 17 Wild Horizon/Universal Images Group/ Getty Images; p. 19 Jason Mintzer/Shutterstock.com.

Printed in the United States of America

CPSIA compliance information: Batch #CW15GS: For further information contact Gareth Stevens, New York, New York at 1-800-542-2595.

CONTENTS

Boldface words appear in the glossary.

What Are Lizards?

Lizards are **reptiles**. They have dry, **scaly** skin. Most have a small head and a short neck. They often have a long body. There are more than 4,600 kinds, or species, of lizards around the world!

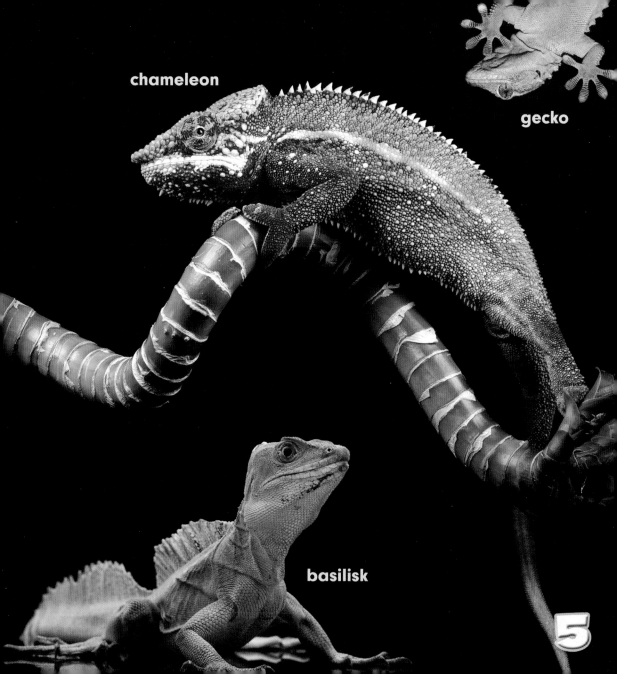

chameleon

gecko

basilisk

5

Some people think lizards are creepy. But everything they do is to **survive**. Lizards are tasty meals for many kinds of animals. So, lizards need to have special **adaptations** to help them stay alive.

7

One Lizard, Many Names

There is one kind of lizard that has a wide, flat body shape, like a toad's body. Its head has **spikes** on it, like horns. Sometimes it's called the horned toad or the short-horned toad. It's also called the horned lizard.

A Nosy Tongue?

Like snakes, lizards smell with their tongue. The horned lizard catches **scents** in the air with its tongue. Then, a body part in the lizard's mouth tells the lizard what the smell is. It knows if a predator or prey is close by.

That's Gross!

Hawks, snakes, and other lizards are some of the horned lizard's predators. When a predator gets too close, some species of horned lizards **squirt** a bloody liquid out of the corners of their eyes! The blood squirts up to 3 feet (0.9 m) away!

13

The horned lizard's predators are usually shocked and surprised by the blood. That gives the lizard a chance to get away. The blood is also harmful to some animals, such as dogs, wolves, and **coyotes**.

15

More Defenses

The horned lizard doesn't often shoot blood out of its eyes, though. Its most common **defense** is to puff itself up. It can grow to be two times its normal size! That can scare some smaller predators away.

Horned lizard skin looks a bit like rocks. This helps the lizard blend in with its rocky desert home. Its spikes also make it look hard to eat to animals like snakes, who would try to swallow it whole.

19

Visit the Lizard

There are about 14 species of horned lizards in Canada, the United States, and Mexico. They mostly live in deserts and dry, warm areas of these countries. If you don't live near horned lizards, you might be able to see one at the zoo!

22

GLOSSARY

adaptation: a change in a type of animal that makes it better able to live in its surroundings

coyote: a meat-eating animal similar to but smaller than a wolf

defense: a way of guarding against an enemy

reptile: an animal covered with scales or plates that breathes air, has a backbone, and lays eggs, such as a turtle, snake, lizard, or crocodile

scaly: describing skin made up of flat plates

scent: smell

spike: a narrow, sharp point

squirt: to force something out of a little opening in a quick stream

survive: to live through something

FOR MORE INFORMATION

BOOKS

Bishop, Nic. *Lizards*. New York, NY: Scholastic, 2010.

Houran, Lori Haskins. *Bloody Horned Lizards*. New York, NY: Bearport Publishing, 2009.

Sirota, Lyn A. *Horned Lizards*. Mankato, MN: Capstone Press, 2010.

WEBSITES

Horned Lizards
www.desertmuseum.org/books/nhsd_horned_lizard.php
Read about this spiky lizard.

Horned Toad (Short-Horned Lizard)
animals.nationalgeographic.com/animals/reptiles/horned-toad/
Find out more about this animal with some misleading names.

INDEX

McLEAN MERCER REGIONAL LIBRARY
BOX 505
RIVERDALE, ND 58565

DATE DUE

			PRINTED IN U.S.A.